Faith Unshaken

A Journey of Trust, Triumph, and Transformation

By
Pastor Henry Owens Jr.

Table Of Content

About the Author

Pastor Henry Owens is a dynamic voice of biblical faith, known for his unwavering commitment to the Word of God and his passionate delivery of truth across generations. With over 40 years of ministerial experience, he currently serves as the Senior Pastor at Word & Spirit Christian Center in Goodyear, Arizona. His calling has taken him across denominational, cultural, and generational lines, equipping believers to walk in unshakable faith.

Ordained at just 12 years old, Pastor Owens was a child prodigy evangelist, preaching throughout Southern California. Since then, he has served in various ministerial roles, including Christian Education Director, youth leader, men's ministry coordinator, marriage counselor, and associate pastor. He and his wife, Latrice, have also served faithfully at Christ Church of the Valley, where they mentor couples and lead small groups.

An educator and visionary, Pastor Owens launched Word & Spirit Christian Academy—an online Bible school designed to train ministers in sound doctrine and spiritual authority. He has authored multiple study guides on eschatology and completed his first film script, *Behold I Come Quickly*, in 2013.

Outside the pulpit, he brings 29 years of experience in telecommunications and is the co-founder of a family trucking business. His personal life is a testimony to God's grace: he is a devoted husband, father of two daughters, and grandfather to seven beloved grandchildren.

With a heart for discipleship, a love for the Scriptures, and a prophetic insight into the times we live in, Pastor Henry Owens continues to challenge, equip, and inspire believers to live a faith that cannot be shaken.

Dedication

I want to dedicate this book to my Lord and Savior, Jesus Christ, the author and finisher of my faith. Without His grace and mercy, this journey would not have been possible.

To my beloved wife, Latrice L. Owens, thank you for your unwavering encouragement, love, and support. You have been my earthly example of faithfulness and strength.

To my daughters, Tatiyanna L. Owens and Brittany M. Owens/Ellis, your love and perseverance inspire me daily.

And to my seven precious granddaughters—Amiyah Jackson, Layanna Ellis, A'sani Ellis, Serenity Ellis, Grace Ellis, Zyiah Ellis, and Zariah Matthews—you bring joy, laughter, and light into my life. May your faith always remain unshaken.

Acknowledgments

I want to acknowledge my Lord and Savior, Jesus Christ. Without His wisdom, none of this would have been possible.

To my wife, Latrice L. Owens, my lifelong partner in love and ministry—you have been my greatest supporter and prayer warrior. To my children, Tatiyanna Owens and Brittany Ellis, and my seven granddaughters—Amiyah, Layanna, A'sani, Serenity, Grace, Zyiah, and Zariah—I love you all dearly.

My spiritual parents, Pastor Glenn & Gwen Taylor of Reno, NV—thank you for decades of encouragement and for helping me cultivate a deeper walk with God.

To Elder Waterford of Los Angeles, CA, thank you for guiding me into ministry and helping me obtain my license. To Minister Bowers, who encouraged me to preach the gospel in my youth, your influence remains with me to this day.

I also want to honor my sisters, Myrdle Broughton, Samantha Butler, and Patricia Owens (who has gone home to be with the Lord), and my mother, Clester Willis-Jefferson, who inspired me to evangelize alongside her twin sister, Vester Moore.

To my brothers in faith and life—Lenard and Monique Dotson, Matthew and Rhonda Knight, Anthony and Loretta Velasquez, Vincent Stewart, Glenn Taylor II, Eddie Butler, Mitchell and Geishula Moore Jr., Terrell and Tara Taylor, and Tabu and Ebony McKnight—thank you for your friendship, prayers, and support throughout this journey of faith.

About the Author

Pastor Henry Owens Jr. grew up in the church as a child prodigy and was called and licensed in the ministry at just twelve years old. With more than four decades of ministry experience, Pastor Owens has faithfully served in multiple churches across the United States in leadership roles that include teaching, pastoral care, and evangelism.

A devoted student of Scripture, he has studied the books of Daniel and Revelation for over thirty years, developing a prophetic understanding of faith and perseverance that has become central to his teaching ministry.

Pastor Owens currently hosts live weekly Bible study sessions on YouTube and Facebook, reaching audiences across the globe with sound doctrine, compassion, and the power of the Holy Spirit.

He has been married to his wife, Latrice L. Owens, for thirty-five years, and together they have two daughters and seven granddaughters. His life's mission is simple yet profound—to help believers stand firm, grow strong, and live with faith unshaken.

Synopsis

When life shakes everything you thought was stable, faith becomes your anchor. In Faith Unshaken, Pastor Henry Owens Jr. invites readers on a powerful journey through Scripture, experience, and revelation—showing how faith can remain firm even when the storms of life rage.

This book isn't about religion—it's about relationship. Through biblical insights, personal testimonies, and divine principles, Pastor Owens reveals how to cultivate faith that does not waver under pressure but grows stronger through adversity.

You will discover:

How to trust God when nothing makes sense.

The role of prayer, patience, and perseverance in sustaining faith.

The dangers of doubt and the discipline of belief.

The connection between obedience, endurance, and spiritual authority.

How to rebuild faith after loss, pain, or disappointment.

Faith Unshaken will remind you that storms don't destroy believers—they define them. Whether you're facing fear, uncertainty, or spiritual fatigue, this book will reignite your confidence in God's promises and help you walk boldly in faith that cannot be moved.

When the world shakes, let your faith stand. When others give up, let your heart believe. When all else fails—trust God, and keep your Faith Unshaken.

Forward

When Pastor Henry Owens first told me that he was writing a book, I was excited because after knowing Henry and his wife Latrice for a little over 30 years, I knew that his book would bless everyone who reads it the same way he and his family has been a blessing to my family and so many others.

I began to read and immediately I was hooked from the very first chapter to the last, faith Unshaken will be a book that I will have in my library at home and in my office at church to draw from its riches from time to time, that is how much I enjoyed reading it and I know you will to.

When I first Heard Henry preach he was a young minister, I knew that God was going to use him in a powerful way, and many would agree that God has and continues to do so, If you ever had the honor to hear Henry preach, teach or speak at your church or one of your conferences like I have, you already know that this God fearing, full of life, exuberant, cheerful, intelligent and funny man of God with a faith that is unshaken, and does not skip a beat when he flows under the power of God's anointing that is over his life.

We had the honor to have Pastor Owens as the Keynote speaker at our 2024 Chosen Men's Conference, once he took the platform he impacted the lives of over 168 men and their families, the response was so great that we invited him back to our conference in 2025 where he was our guest pastor speaker and once again his insight and ability to teach the word of God was powerful and well received.

When Henry asked me if I would foreword his new book, I felt extremely humble, honored and blessed, I'm excited to share with you what I already knew was going to be an amazing book.

Faith Unshaken: Unlocking the Power of Faith. Immediately after the first chapter I went on to the next and I thought, before you can get to a treasure chest you must first discover it; and after discovering it you must then unlock it to benefit from its hidden treasures, sometimes that treasure chest just sits buried with all of life's circumstances until one unlocks it and rediscovers it's riches, Henry does just that with his book that you now hold in your hand, Reading this book, I believe will help a new or current believer to discover and unlock the power that is sure to help them grow more in their faith and if you are a pastor or church leader you can draw from it, be encouraged and power up the faith you already have by increasing your potential to have faith like Jesus. This book can help you to teach others about Faith with what could easily become a sermon series.

I found Faith Unshaken to be an easy read and in it a memorization pattern that Henry uses starting with Biblical Examples which he comes back to with different views that unlock the treasures found in the scripture in an easy-to-understand commentary form in his own words, my favorite being and I quote from this great book "without faith , no one can please God, receive His grace, or enter into eternal life" that's Pure fire right there! Amen

In The Key Questions Answered, I personally enjoy the bullet point questions that Henry moves to answer by giving practical application examples with scripture and verse that one might know, but does not put into practice like they should. The Biblical Examples followed by the application makes it easier to walk by faith when a person follows what the bible teaches about faith; and Henry does an outstanding job in showing the reader how to stay on track and do just that. Faith Unshaken: Unlocking the Power of Faith what a powerful book that every leader should have in their arsenal, after reading this book it was like a Supernatural Energy Drink that literally gave a boost to my faith.

From the historic to present time testimonies Faith Unshaken is sure to inspire. I highly recommend this book, buy it as a gift for yourself and others because no matter where you are in your faith journey, Faith Unshaken will help you unlock more faith Power and have you Living In Faith Every day which pleases God.

Anthony Velazquez

Founding Pastor, Life Ministries LM

Founder, Chosen Men's Conference

Clinton Missouri.

Faith Unshaken: Unlocking the Power of Faith

Opening: Why This Book Matters

Faith is more than just a religious concept—it is the key that unlocks the power of God in our lives. Without faith, we cannot please God, walk in His promises, or experience the fullness of His blessings. The Bible tells us that faith is the substance of things hoped for and the evidence of things unseen (*Hebrews 11:1*). But what does that truly mean?

Many people believe in God, but few understand how to live by faith. True faith moves mountains, heals the sick, calls things that are not as though they were, and brings the impossible into reality. This book will guide you through a deep biblical journey, showing you how to strengthen your faith, activate the promises of God, and live a victorious life.

📖 Did you know that faith is a law, just like gravity? It operates on spiritual principles that, when understood and applied, produce supernatural results.

📖 Did you know that Jesus rebuked His disciples more for their lack of faith than for any other sin? That's because faith is the bridge between heaven and earth, the key to unlocking God's miracles in your life.

📖 Have you ever wondered why some prayers go unanswered? The Bible teaches that faith-filled prayers are the ones that move God's hand.

This book is for every believer who desires to go beyond surface-level Christianity and step into a life of unshaken faith—the kind of faith that stops storms, raises the dead, and brings divine provision. Whether you are new to faith or have been walking with God for years, these 12 chapters will give you a deeper understanding of biblical faith and how to apply it to every area of your life.

Are you ready to unlock the supernatural power of faith? Let's begin!

Chapter 1:
What Is Faith?

📖 *Hebrews 11:1* – "Now faith is the substance of things hoped for, the evidence of things not seen."

Faith is the foundation of a believer's life—it is the bridge between the natural and the supernatural, the physical and the spiritual. Without faith, it is impossible to please God (*Hebrews 11:6*). Faith is more than mere belief; it is **active trust in God** that manifests through obedience, perseverance, and action.

Key Questions Answered:

- What does the Bible say about faith?
- How does faith differ from belief?
- Why is faith essential in a Christian's life?

Faith is the spiritual currency of the Kingdom of God. It is not wishful thinking or blind optimism—faith is anchored in the truth of God's Word. Faith is seeing with spiritual eyes what has not yet manifested in the physical world but is promised by God.

What Does the Bible Say About Faith?

The Bible defines faith as the substance of things hoped for, the evidence of things not seen (*Hebrews 11:1*). This means that faith is not abstract—it is tangible in the spiritual realm and brings reality into the physical world.

Faith Is a Requirement, Not an Option

📖 *Hebrews 11:6* – "Without faith, it is impossible to please God, because anyone who comes to Him must believe that He exists and that He rewards those who earnestly seek Him."

Faith is the foundation of a relationship with God. We cannot see Him with our natural eyes, yet we trust in His existence and His promises. From the beginning of time, God has required faith from His people. Every interaction between God and man has been based on trust in His word.

📖 Biblical Example: Noah (*Genesis 6:13-22*) ✅ God commanded Noah to build an ark because a flood was coming, even though it had never rained before. Noah's faith in God's word saved his family and preserved mankind.

Faith vs. Belief: What's the Difference?

Many people **believe in God** but do not **live by faith**. Even demons believe in God and tremble (*James 2:19*), but faith goes beyond belief—it requires action, trust, and commitment.

📖 *James 2:17* – "Faith by itself, if it is not accompanied by action, is dead."

Belief acknowledges something as true, but faith **acts upon that truth**. Faith is demonstrated in how we live, pray, and obey God's commands.

📖 **Biblical Example:** The Woman with the Issue of Blood (*Mark 5:25-34*) ✅ She **believed** Jesus could heal her, but she **acted** in faith by reaching out to touch His garment. Her faith made her whole.

Faith moves us from **passive acknowledgment to active trust**. It leads us to take bold steps, knowing that God will fulfill His promises.

Why Is Faith Essential in a Christian's Life?

Faith is the **spiritual force** that enables believers to receive from God, live victoriously, and fulfill their purpose. Without faith, our prayers are ineffective, our relationship with God is stagnant, and our spiritual growth is hindered.

1. Faith Connects Us to God's Promises

📖 *2 Corinthians 5:7* – "For we walk by faith, not by sight."

Faith is how we **receive salvation, healing, provision, and every other blessing** in God's kingdom. It allows us to stand firm even when circumstances contradict God's promises.

📖 **Biblical Example:** Abraham's Call (*Genesis 12:1-4*) ✅ God told Abraham to leave his homeland without knowing where he was going. Abraham's faith led him to become the father of many nations.

2. Faith Enables Miracles

📖 *Matthew 17:20* – "If you have faith as small as a mustard seed, you can say to this mountain, 'Move from here to there,' and it will move."

Faith is the **power behind every miracle** in the Bible. Jesus often told people, "Your faith has made you well." Healing, deliverance, and provision are all activated by faith.

📖 **Biblical Example:** The Centurion's Servant (*Matthew 8:5-13*) ✅ The centurion believed Jesus could heal his servant **just by speaking a word**. Jesus marveled at his faith and granted his request.

3. Faith Protects Us from Fear and Doubt

📖 *Isaiah 41:10* – "Do not fear, for I am with you."

Faith and fear **cannot coexist**. When we trust in God, we reject fear and stand firm in His promises.

📖 **Biblical Example:** David vs. Goliath (*1 Samuel 17*) ✅ While others saw a giant, David **saw God's power**. His faith led to victory.

Faith as the Activating Force of the Believer

Faith is the force that moves the believer from merely hoping to **knowing and declaring** the promises of God. Faith **calls things that are not as though they were**, bringing supernatural realities into existence (*Romans 4:17*).

📖 **Biblical Example:** God's Creation Power (*Genesis 1*) ✅ God **spoke the world into existence**, demonstrating that faith is declared before manifestation.

Practical Application: Activating Faith in Daily Life

1. **Speak the Word** – Confession of faith aligns your words with God's will (*Mark 11:23*).

2. **Act on God's Promises** – Step out in faith, even when circumstances seem impossible (*James 2:26*).
3. **Resist Doubt** – Stand firm in faith, rejecting fear and unbelief (*Ephesians 6:16*).
4. **Stay Rooted in Scripture** – Faith grows by hearing and applying God's Word (*Romans 10:17*).

📖 **Personal Reflection:** What areas of your life require more faith? Are you acting on God's promises, or simply believing without stepping forward?

Conclusion: Faith Is the Foundation of Victory

Faith is not just believing that God can—it is knowing that He will. It is the bridge between the unseen and the seen, the spiritual and the physical. Living by faith unlocks miracles, divine provision, and supernatural breakthroughs.

📖 *1 John 5:4* – "For everyone born of God overcomes the world. This is the victory that has overcome the world, even our faith."

Faith is the victory. It is the key to unlocking everything God has for you. The question is: Will you step out in faith and believe God's promises, or will you settle for a life limited by doubt?

📖 **Prayer for Faith:** "Father, I thank You that faith is the key to walking in Your promises. Help me to trust You completely, to step out in obedience, and to believe in the impossible. Strengthen my faith and remove every doubt that hinders me from living the life You have called me to. In Jesus' name, Amen."

Chapter 2:
Faith vs. Belief—What's the Difference?

📖 *James 2:19* – "You believe that there is one God. Good! Even the demons believe that—and shudder."

Many **believe** in God, but **faith** is trusting and acting on that belief. Faith is more than intellectual acknowledgment—it is a commitment to live according to what one believes. A person can believe in God's existence without having a transformative relationship with Him. Faith requires not only **knowing** but **trusting** and **acting** on what God has revealed.

Key Questions Answered:

- How is faith different from belief?
- Why isn't belief enough?
- How can we turn belief into faith?

Belief accepts that something is true. Faith **takes action** upon that belief. Even demons believe in God's existence but do not serve Him. Faith is demonstrated by obedience, trust, and endurance.

📖 Biblical Example: Peter Walking on Water (*Matthew 14:28-31*) ✅ Peter believed in Jesus enough to step out onto the water, but when doubt crept in, his faith wavered, and he began to sink. This moment teaches us that faith is not just stepping out—it is remaining steadfast even when trials come.

📖 *James 2:17* – "Faith by itself, if it is not accompanied by action, is dead."

Understanding the Depth of Faith vs. Belief

1. Belief Recognizes; Faith Acts

Belief alone does not produce transformation. Faith requires stepping out, trusting in God's ability, and moving forward even when we do not see the full picture.

📖 Biblical Example: The Israelites at the Red Sea (*Exodus 14:21-22*) ✅ They believed God could deliver them, but it was only when they stepped into the sea that it parted. Many today say they believe in God's promises but fail to take the steps required to see those promises fulfilled.

2. Belief Can Coexist with Doubt; Faith Resists Doubt

Belief may acknowledge God's power, but faith holds onto His promises **without wavering**. Doubt weakens belief, while faith stands firm.

📖 Biblical Example: Thomas the Doubter (*John 20:24-29*) ✅ Thomas believed only after seeing Jesus resurrected. Jesus responded, *"Blessed are those who have not seen and yet have believed."* This underscores that faith operates without needing evidence.

3. Faith Requires Complete Trust in God

Faith operates beyond what the natural senses perceive.

📖 *2 Corinthians 5:7* – "For we walk by faith, not by sight."

Faith is trusting in God's Word above all circumstances. If we are waiting for visible proof before we trust God, we are not operating in faith.

📖 Biblical Example: Abraham Offering Isaac (*Genesis 22:1-18*) ✔️ Abraham was willing to sacrifice Isaac because he had faith in God's ability to provide. He did not understand how God would fulfill His promise, but he knew God would. Faith trusts before the outcome is revealed.

4. Faith Moves Beyond Human Logic

Belief may require reasoning, but faith surpasses logic and moves according to God's Word.

📖 Biblical Example: The Walls of Jericho (*Joshua 6:1-20*) ✔️ Walking around a city and shouting does not seem logical for battle, but faith brought victory. Many times, God's commands require obedience before understanding.

How to Develop Faith Beyond Belief

1. **Hearing the Word of God** (*Romans 10:17*)

o   Faith comes by hearing the Word and **meditating on it**.

o   The more we immerse ourselves in Scripture, the stronger our faith becomes.

2. **Acting on What You Believe** (*James 1:22*)

o   Move from passive belief to active trust.

o   Faith is proven by obedience. God rewards those who act upon what He has said.

3. **Speaking in Faith** (*Mark 11:23*)

o Declare God's promises over your life.

o Our words shape our faith. Speaking doubt weakens our trust in God's promises.

4. **Standing Firm in Trials** (*James 1:3*)

o Trials refine faith, producing perseverance.

o Faith is tested in difficulty, and enduring hardship builds spiritual strength.

5. **Rejecting Fear and Doubt** (*Isaiah 41:10*)

o Fear undermines faith. Stand firm in God's truth.

o The enemy tries to plant fear, but faith requires resisting those thoughts with the Word of God.

6. **Prayer and Fasting** (*Mark 9:29*)

o Some spiritual breakthroughs only come through **deep communion with God**.

o Faith grows when we dedicate time to seeking God.

7. **Surround Yourself with Faithful People** (*Proverbs 27:17*)

o "As iron sharpens iron, so one person sharpens another."

o Who you spend time with will **either build or weaken** your faith.

Faith in Action: How Real Faith Transforms Lives

Faith is not only about receiving from God but also about pleasing Him.

📖 *Hebrews 11:6* – "Without faith, it is impossible to please God."

Faith activates the supernatural. Miracles occur when faith is present. Throughout Scripture, Jesus often emphasized that people's faith was the key to their breakthrough.

📖 Biblical Example: The Woman with the Issue of Blood (*Mark 5:25-34*) ✅ She believed in Jesus' power, but her faith was demonstrated when she pressed through the crowd and touched His garment. Her faith made her whole.

📖 Biblical Example: The Centurion's Faith (*Matthew 8:5-13*) ✅ The centurion believed Jesus could heal his servant, but his faith was evident when he told Jesus He didn't need to come in person—He only needed to speak the word. Jesus marveled at his great faith.

📖 Conclusion: Moving from Belief to Faith Belief is the starting point, but faith is what brings results. Faith is what allows us to receive salvation, walk in victory, and see the impossible happen.

📖 *Hebrews 10:38* – "The righteous shall live by faith."

Faith is not a momentary decision—it is a lifestyle. It is trusting in God's promises, stepping out in obedience, and standing firm even when the answer is delayed. The greatest victories in life come through faith.

📖 Final Reflection:

- Do you have belief without faith?
- Are you actively stepping out in obedience to God's Word?

- Are you growing your faith daily through prayer, Scripture, and action?

Faith is the difference between seeing God's power in theory and seeing it at work in your life. Make the decision today to walk in faith!

Chapter 3:
Faith Comes by Hearing

📖 *Romans 10:17* – "So then faith comes by hearing, and hearing by the word of God."

Faith does not originate from within us—it comes by receiving the Word of God. The more we hear and absorb God's Word, the stronger our faith becomes. Faith is not automatic—it must be cultivated.

Understanding How Faith Grows

Faith is **like a seed**—it needs to be planted, watered, and nurtured before it grows (*Matthew 13:3-9*). Hearing the Word of God repeatedly allows the seed of faith to take root and bear fruit in our lives.

Key Questions Answered:

- How does faith grow?
- Why is hearing God's Word essential?
- How can we actively build our faith?

Faith is developed through exposure to truth. If we are constantly surrounded by doubt, negativity, and fear, our faith weakens. However, when we **immerse ourselves in God's promises**, faith flourishes.

📖 Biblical Example: The Roman Centurion's Faith (*Luke 7:1-10*) ✅ He believed in Jesus' authority without needing physical evidence. He simply heard of Jesus' power and took Him at His

Word. Jesus declared that the Centurion had greater faith than anyone in Israel!

📖 *Hebrews 11:6* – "Without faith, it is impossible to please God."

How Hearing Builds Faith

1. Hearing the Word Produces Belief

o   You cannot trust someone you do not know.

o   The more we **hear about God**, the more we trust Him.

2. Hearing the Word Replaces Fear with Faith

o   The enemy constantly feeds us fear and doubt.

o   When we hear the truth of Scripture, it replaces those lies.

3. Hearing the Word Activates the Promises of God

o   God's promises become real when we **declare them in faith**.

o   Confessing Scripture aligns our words with God's power (*Mark 11:23*).

📖 Biblical Example: Jesus Teaching the Disciples (*Mark 4:35-41*) ✅ The disciples heard Jesus' teachings, but when a storm came, they panicked. Jesus expected them to apply what they had heard.

Practical Application: Speaking and Confessing the Word Builds Faith

Faith is activated when we speak God's Word. Our words shape our reality—they either bring life or death (*Proverbs 18:21*).

13

1. Speak the Word Over Your Life

📖 *Joshua 1:8* – "Keep this Book of the Law always on your lips; meditate on it day and night."

- When we speak Scripture, our minds are renewed.
- Declaring God's promises builds faith in our spirit.

2. Call Things into Existence Through Faith

📖 *Romans 4:17* – "God calls things that are not as though they were."

- Faith-filled speech aligns our reality with God's will.
- The Bible is full of people who spoke in faith before seeing results.

📖 Biblical Example: Ezekiel Prophesying to Dry Bones (Ezekiel 37:1-10) ✅ Ezekiel spoke God's Word over lifeless bones, and they came to life.

3. Surround Yourself with Faith-Filled Teaching

📖 *Proverbs 27:17* – "As iron sharpens iron, so one person sharpens another."

- Listen to sermons, worship, and faith-filled conversations.
- Eliminate voices of doubt and fear.

Hindrances to Faith Growth

Even when we hear God's Word, obstacles can block faith from growing.

1. Doubt and Unbelief

📖 *James 1:6-7* – "But when you ask, you must believe and not doubt."

• Doubt weakens faith, making it ineffective.
• We must actively reject thoughts of unbelief.

2. Fear and Negative Speech

📖 *2 Timothy 1:7* – "For God has not given us a spirit of fear."

• Fear contradicts faith. The more we speak fear, the more we suppress faith.

3. Lack of the Word

📖 *Hosea 4:6* – "My people are destroyed for lack of knowledge."

• A faithless life is a Word-less life. We must consume Scripture daily.

Faith in Action: How Hearing the Word Transforms Lives

Faith is more than just listening—it requires acting on what we hear (*James 1:22*).

📖 Biblical Example: The Woman with the Issue of Blood (*Mark 5:25-34*) ✓ She heard about Jesus, and it stirred faith within her. She acted on that faith and was healed.

📖 Biblical Example: Blind Bartimaeus (*Mark 10:46-52*) ✓ He heard that Jesus was near and called out in faith. His faith led to his sight being restored.

Steps to Strengthen Faith Through Hearing

1. **Read the Bible Daily**

o   Meditate on God's promises.

2. **Listen to Faith-Building Messages**

o   Surround yourself with anointed teachings.

3. **Confess Scripture Out Loud**

o   Speak the Word over your circumstances.

4. **Pray the Word**

o   Pray using God's promises.

5. **Reject Words of Doubt and Fear**

o   Cancel negativity with God's truth.

6. **Engage in Faith Conversations**

o   Speak with others who encourage and build up your faith.

7. **Practice Gratitude and Praise**

o   Worship strengthens faith and shifts focus onto God.

Real-Life Testimonies of Faith Growing Through Hearing

📖 Modern Testimony: A woman diagnosed with terminal illness was given six months to live. She immersed herself in hearing the Word daily, listening to healing scriptures, and speaking life over her body. Her faith led to her complete healing, baffling doctors.

📖 Historical Testimony: George Müller, known for running orphanages, never asked anyone for financial support. Instead, he

16

heard the Word, prayed in faith, and saw God provide miraculously for thousands of children.

📖 Conclusion: Faith Grows by Hearing and Applying the Word

Faith is not automatic—it grows when we actively hear, receive, and apply God's Word. The more we listen to His promises, the stronger our faith becomes.

📖 *Hebrews 10:38* – "The righteous shall live by faith."

Will you choose to hear and obey God's Word today?

Faith begins where the Word of God is heard—so let us listen, declare, and act in faith!

Chapter 4:
Faith Without Works Is Dead

📖 *James 2:26* – "For as the body without the spirit is dead, so faith without works is dead also."

Faith is not just **believing**—it must be demonstrated through **actions**. Faith that does not move is **inactive and ineffective**. Scripture shows that faith must be combined with **obedience** for it to bear fruit.

Faith Must Be Demonstrated Through Action

Faith is more than just a mental agreement with God's Word; it must be followed by **works** that reflect that faith.

📖 **Biblical Example:** Rahab's Faith in Action (*Joshua 2:1-21*)
✅ Rahab **believed** in the power of God, but she proved her faith by **hiding the Israelite spies** and aligning herself with God's people. Because of her actions, she and her family were saved.

📖 *James 2:17* – "Faith by itself, if it is not accompanied by action, is dead."

Understanding Faith's Power

1. **Faith Requires Movement**

o Faith is active, not passive.

o A person who truly believes will take steps that reflect that belief.

2. Jesus Required Action Before Miracles Happened

o Faith always requires a corresponding action.

o Jesus often instructed people to **do something** before their miracles occurred.

📖 **Biblical Example:** The Lame Man at the Pool of Bethesda (*John 5:1-9*) ✅ Jesus told him to **pick up his mat and walk** before he was healed. The man had to **act in faith** to receive his miracle.

📖 Biblical Example: The Ten Lepers (*Luke 17:11-19*) ✅ Jesus told them to go show themselves to the priest, and as they went, they were healed. Their faith was demonstrated through obedience.

How to Put Faith into Action

1. Obedience to God's Word

📖 *Luke 6:46* – "Why do you call me 'Lord, Lord,' and do not do what I say?"

• True faith results in **obedience** to God's commands.
• If we say we believe in God, our actions must align with that belief.

2. Speaking and Declaring in Faith

📖 *Mark 11:23* – "Truly I tell you, if anyone says to this mountain, 'Go, throw yourself into the sea,' and does not doubt in their heart but believes that what they say will happen, it will be done for them."

- Faith must be spoken and declared.
- Our words must align with what we believe.

3. Taking Bold Steps of Faith

📖 *2 Corinthians 5:7* – "For we walk by faith, not by sight."

- Faith means taking steps even when we do not see the outcome yet.
- Abraham left his homeland without knowing where he was going (*Hebrews 11:8*).

📖 Biblical Example: Peter Walking on Water (*Matthew 14:28-31*) ✅ Peter stepped out of the boat before the water held him up. The miracle only happened after he moved in faith.

Faith Without Works Cannot Bear Fruit

Many people struggle in their walk with God because their faith is **not backed by action**.

1. Faith Without Works Is Empty

📖 *Titus 1:16* – "They claim to know God, but by their actions, they deny him."

- Many **believe in God** but do not live in a way that reflects their faith.
- If faith does not affect your actions, it is not real faith.

2. True Faith Produces Obedience

📖 *John 14:15* – "If you love me, keep my commands."

- Faith and love for God are shown through **obedience**.

- Abraham proved his faith when he **offered Isaac** on the altar (*Genesis 22:1-18*).

📖 Biblical Example: Noah Building the Ark (*Hebrews 11:7*) ✅ Noah had never seen rain, yet he spent years building an ark because he believed God's warning. His faith was proven through his works.

Practical Steps to Activate Your Faith

1. Step Out in Obedience

o   Move when God says move.

o   Don't wait to "feel ready."

2. Speak God's Promises Over Your Life

o   Replace fear with declarations of faith.

o   Speak life over your situations.

3. Serve Others and Show Christ's Love

o   Faith without **love** is incomplete (*Galatians 5:6*).

4. Pray and Expect God to Answer

o   Pray with faith, not doubt.

o   Thank God **before** the answer comes (*Philippians 4:6*).

5. Give and Trust God to Provide

o   Giving is an act of faith (*Luke 6:38*).

Faith in Action: How Works Demonstrate Faith

📖 Biblical Example: The Friends Who Lowered the Paralytic Through the Roof (*Mark 2:1-12*) ✅ They did not just believe Jesus could heal—they took action by tearing a hole in the roof and lowering their friend down to Jesus. Jesus saw their faith and healed the man.

📖 Biblical Example: The Widow at Zarephath (*1 Kings 17:8-16*) ✔ She gave her last bit of flour to the prophet Elijah before she saw the miracle of provision. Faith acted first.

Real-Life Testimonies of Faith With Works

📖 Modern Testimony: A man believed God for a new job but did not apply anywhere. Once he stepped out in faith and started submitting applications, the right job was offered to him. Faith without action is ineffective.

📖 Historical Testimony: Missionary Hudson Taylor moved to China with no financial backing. He trusted God fully and saw miracles of provision because he acted on his faith.

📖 Conclusion: Faith Without Works Is Dead

📖 Hebrews 10:38 – "The righteous shall live by faith."

Faith is not just believing—it is acting on that belief. If we truly trust God, we will obey His Word, take bold steps, and allow our faith to guide our decisions.

📖 James 1:22 – "Do not merely listen to the word, and so deceive yourselves. Do what it says."

Faith requires movement, obedience, and action. Are you demonstrating your faith through works?

Faith that moves produces miracles, blessings, and transformation—but it must be activated through obedience and action.

Faith Unshaken: Unlocking the Power of Biblical Faith

Chapter 5:
Trials Test and Strengthen Faith

📖 *James 1:3* – "Because you know that the testing of your faith produces perseverance."

Faith is not proven in moments of ease but in times of **testing and hardship**. Trials refine our faith, much like fire refines gold, burning away impurities and revealing a faith that is strong, unwavering, and built on the foundation of God's promises.

Faith Is Strengthened Through Challenges

Faith that is never tested remains weak. True faith is **developed through trials** because challenges push us closer to God and teach us to trust in His provision and timing.

📖 **Biblical Example:** Job's Faith in Suffering (*Job 1-42*) ✅ Despite losing his wealth, health, and family, Job **remained faithful** to God. His perseverance led to a greater restoration than he had before.

📖 *1 Peter 1:7* – "These have come so that the proven genuineness of your faith—of greater worth than gold—may result in praise, glory, and honor when Jesus Christ is revealed."

Faith Under Fire: The Purpose of Testing

1. Trials Strengthen Our Trust in God

o When everything is going well, faith is easy. When trials come, we are forced to **rely fully on God**.

o **Faith is built in the fire**—it does not grow in comfort.

2. Challenges Produce Perseverance

o Every great man or woman of faith faced **difficult circumstances** before walking in God's promises.

o If we give up in the face of trials, our faith remains stagnant.

📖 **Biblical Example:** Abraham and Isaac (*Genesis 22:1-14*) ✅ Abraham's faith was **tested** when God asked him to sacrifice Isaac. Because he obeyed, God provided a ram as a substitute, proving that faith leads to **divine provision**.

How to Endure Trials With Faith

1. Stand on God's Promises

📖 *Isaiah 41:10* – "Do not fear, for I am with you; do not be dismayed, for I am your God. I will strengthen you and help you."

• Trials make us feel **abandoned**, but God never leaves us.
• Memorizing and **declaring** God's promises helps us remain strong.

2. Keep Praying and Trusting God

📖 *Philippians 4:6-7* – "Do not be anxious about anything, but in every situation, by prayer and petition, with thanksgiving, present your requests to God."

- Faith is strengthened when we keep praying, even when we **don't see answers immediately**.
- Trusting in God's timing brings **peace**.

3. Worship in the Storm

📖 *Acts 16:25-26* – "About midnight Paul and Silas were praying and singing hymns to God, and the other prisoners were listening to them. Suddenly there was such a violent earthquake that the foundations of the prison were shaken."

- Worship shifts our focus from our **problems** to God's **power**.
- Paul and Silas **praised God in chains**, and He set them free.

Faith-Based Declarations Sustain Believers

📖 *Mark 11:24* – "Whatever you ask for in prayer, believe that you have received it, and it will be yours."

1. **Declare Victory Before You See It**

o Faith sees **beyond the natural**.

o Speak life even when circumstances look hopeless.

📖 **Biblical Example:** The Shunammite Woman (*2 Kings 4:8-37*) ✓ Even after her son died, she said, *"It is well."* Her faith resulted in his resurrection.

2. **Refuse to Speak Fear and Doubt**

o **Doubt cancels faith**. Be mindful of what you confess.

o Speak only what aligns with God's Word.

📖 *Proverbs 18:21* – "The tongue has the power of life and death."

3. **Hold Onto God's Promises Even When It's Hard**

o Faith is not about **feelings**—it is about **truth**.

o Do not let circumstances shake your confidence in God.

📖 Biblical Example: Joseph's Journey (*Genesis 37-50*) ✅ Joseph was betrayed, enslaved, and imprisoned, but he never lost faith in God's promises. His trial led to his greatest blessing.

Practical Steps to Strengthen Faith in Trials

1. **Meditate on Scripture Daily**

o Fill your mind with truth, not fear.

2. **Surround Yourself With Faith-Filled People**

o Find people who encourage, not discourage, your faith.

3. **Refuse to Quit When It Gets Hard**

o God does His greatest work in moments when we feel like giving up.

4. **Write Down Your Testimonies**

o Remember how God has helped you in the past.

Faith in Action: How Trials Produce Miracles

📖 Biblical Example: The Israelites at the Red Sea (*Exodus 14:21-31*) ✅ They were trapped between Pharaoh's army and the sea, but Moses' faith caused the waters to part.

📖 Biblical Example: Elijah and the Widow (*1 Kings 17:8-16*) ✅ She gave Elijah her last meal, and God multiplied her food for the entire famine.

Modern-Day Testimonies of Faith Through Trials

📖 Real-Life Testimony: A woman lost her job but continued tithing and trusting God. Within weeks, she was given a better position with double her previous salary.

📖 Historical Testimony: Corrie ten Boom, who survived the Holocaust, said, *"Never be afraid to trust an unknown future to a known God."* Her faith remained unshaken, and she impacted millions.

📖 Conclusion: Trials Test and Strengthen Faith

📖 *Hebrews 10:38* – "The righteous shall live by faith."

Trials are not a sign that God has abandoned us—they are opportunities for faith to grow stronger. The greatest breakthroughs come after seasons of testing.

📖 *James 1:12* – "Blessed is the one who perseveres under trial because, having stood the test, that person will receive the crown of life."

God is faithful in every storm. Are you standing firm in faith?

Trials produce perseverance, character, and deeper trust in God—but only if we choose to stand strong, trust His Word, and keep pressing forward in faith.

Chapter 6:
Walking by Faith, Not by Sight

📖 *2 Corinthians 5:7* – "For we walk by faith, not by sight."

Faith requires trusting God beyond what we see. It means relying on His promises even when circumstances seem impossible. Many believers struggle because they only trust what they can see and understand, but true faith operates beyond the natural realm.

The Challenge of Walking by Faith

Faith is not based on human logic or what the eyes perceive. It is trusting in the unseen and standing firm on God's truth.

📖 Biblical Example: The Israelites Crossing the Red Sea (*Exodus 14*) ✓ The Israelites had no visible way forward. Yet, Moses stretched out his staff in faith, and the sea parted. They had to step forward before seeing the full deliverance of God.

📖 *Hebrews 11:1* – "Now faith is the substance of things hoped for, the evidence of things not seen."

Faith Transforms Unseen Spiritual Realities into Visible Manifestations

1. **Faith Sees the Invisible**

o   Faith is the **evidence** of what we cannot yet see.

o   It pulls **God's promises** into reality.

2. **Faith Speaks Before It Sees**

o   Faith-filled believers declare victory **before** it happens.

o   God calls things **that are not as though they were** (*Romans 4:17*).

📖 Biblical Example: Joshua and the Walls of Jericho (*Joshua 6:1-20*) ✅ The Israelites marched around the walls of Jericho for seven days before seeing them fall. Faith required obedience first.

How to Walk by Faith Daily

1. Trust God's Word Over Your Circumstances

📖 *Isaiah 55:11* – "So shall my word be that goes out from my mouth; it shall not return to me empty."

- Circumstances change, but God's Word remains true.
- Feelings and situations should never override God's promises.

2. Obey Even When You Don't Understand

📖 *Proverbs 3:5-6* – "Trust in the Lord with all your heart and lean not on your own understanding."

- Walking by faith means following **God's direction**, even when it doesn't make sense.

📖 Biblical Example: Peter Walking on Water (*Matthew 14:28-31*) ✅ Peter walked on water because he trusted Jesus. But when he looked at the waves, he sank. Faith must stay focused on Christ, not circumstances.

Faith in Action: Declaring Before Seeing

📖 *Mark 11:23* – "Truly I tell you, if anyone says to this mountain, 'Go, throw yourself into the sea,' and does not doubt in their heart but believes that what they say will happen, it will be done for them."

1. Speak Victory Over Your Life

- Declare God's promises even when things look impossible.
- Faith-filled words align with God's will.

📖 **Biblical Example:** Ezekiel Prophesying to Dry Bones (*Ezekiel 37:1-10*) ✅ Ezekiel spoke God's Word over dead bones, and **they came to life**.

2. Walk Forward in Obedience

📖 *2 Corinthians 4:18* – "We fix our eyes not on what is seen, but on what is unseen."

- Obedience precedes manifestation.
- Move forward in faith even if the outcome is not yet visible.

📖 Biblical Example: The Widow's Oil (*2 Kings 4:1-7*) ✅ She poured out oil in faith, and God multiplied it beyond what she imagined.

Obstacles to Walking by Faith

1. **Fear and Doubt**

o Fear contradicts faith.

o If Peter had kept his eyes on Jesus, he would not have sunk.

📖 *2 Timothy 1:7* – "For God has not given us a spirit of fear."

2. Relying on Sight Instead of Trusting God

o   Many miss their **breakthrough** because they only believe what they can see.

o   Faith **requires stepping out** even before we see results.

📖 Biblical Example: Gideon (*Judges 6-7*) ✅ Gideon had to believe that God could defeat an entire army with just 300 men.

Practical Steps to Strengthen Your Faith Walk

1. Read and Meditate on God's Word Daily

o   Faith is strengthened by **constant exposure** to truth.

2. Surround Yourself With Faith Builders

o   Stay connected to **strong believers** who encourage your faith.

3. Step Out in Obedience

o   Faith is action-oriented—**take bold steps** even when uncertain.

4. Pray and Speak Life Daily

o   Speak **God's promises** over your life and circumstances.

Faith in Action: Modern-Day Testimonies

📖 Real-Life Testimony: A man diagnosed with terminal illness refused to accept fear. He continually declared healing scriptures over his life. He was miraculously healed, baffling doctors.

📖 Historical Testimony: George Müller ran orphanages without asking anyone for money. He relied only on prayer and faith, and God provided every need.

📖 Conclusion: Walking by Faith Brings Supernatural Results

📖 *Hebrews 10:38* – "The righteous shall live by faith."

Faith is trusting God's plan even when we cannot see it. If we only move when things are visible, we are not walking in faith.

📖 *Romans 8:24-25* – "For in this hope we were saved. But hope that is seen is no hope at all. Who hopes for what they already have?"

Faith sees the unseen, speaks the impossible, and trusts beyond logic. Are you willing to walk by faith, not by sight?

Chapter 7:
Faith the Size of a Mustard Seed

📖 *Matthew 17:20* – "If you have faith as small as a mustard seed, you can say to this mountain, 'Move from here to there,' and it will move."

Faith does not need to be big, but it must be genuine. The power of faith is not in its size but in its source—God Himself. Jesus teaches that even a tiny amount of faith can produce miraculous results if it is placed in Him.

The Strength of Small Faith

Many people believe they need great faith to see results, but Jesus taught that even the smallest faith can move mountains when it is focused on God's power.

📖 Biblical Example: The Bleeding Woman's Faith (*Mark 5:25-34*) ✓ This woman had only a mustard-seed-sized faith—she believed that touching Jesus' garment would heal her. Because of her faith, she was instantly healed.

📖 *Luke 17:6* – "If you have faith as small as a mustard seed, you can say to this mulberry tree, 'Be uprooted and planted in the sea,' and it will obey you."

Understanding Mustard Seed Faith

1. Small Faith, Big God

o Faith is not about how much we have, but who we trust.

o A tiny seed of faith is powerful because God is limitless.

2. Faith Grows Over Time

o Like a mustard seed, faith starts small but grows as it is cultivated.

o Faith increases when **we act on it**.

📖 Biblical Example: The Disciples' Growing Faith (*Luke 8:22-25*) ✅ When Jesus calmed the storm, He asked the disciples, *"Where is your faith?"* Their faith needed growth, but even their small trust in Him led to a miracle.

How to Activate Mustard Seed Faith

1. Believe in God's Power, Not Your Own

📖 *Mark 9:23* – "Everything is possible for one who believes."

• Faith is not about feelings; it is about trust.
• Even when we feel weak, faith says, "God is able."

2. Speak Faith, Not Doubt

📖 *Proverbs 18:21* – "The tongue has the power of life and death."

• What we speak reflects what we believe.
• Speak life and faith over your situations.

📖 Biblical Example: David Facing Goliath (1 Samuel 17:45-47) ✓ David declared victory before he fought Goliath. His faith-filled words activated God's power.

The Power of Acting on Small Faith

📖 *James 2:17* – "Faith by itself, if it is not accompanied by action, is dead."

1. **Faith Requires a Step Forward**

o   Faith grows when we **act on what we believe**.

o   Even small actions of faith lead to **big results**.

📖 **Biblical Example:** The Widow's Flour and Oil (*1 Kings 17:8-16*) ✓ She had only a little food but **acted in faith** by making Elijah a meal first. **Her oil never ran out.**

2. **Faith Is Strengthened Through Use**

o   **Unused faith weakens** over time.

o   When we **step out**, we see faith **multiply**.

📖 Biblical Example: The Ten Lepers (*Luke 17:11-19*) ✓ Jesus told them to go show themselves to the priest. As they went, they were healed. Faith moved before the miracle came.

Obstacles to Growing Faith

1. **Doubt and Fear**

o   **Doubt cancels faith**.

o   Fear keeps believers **from taking steps** of faith.

📖 *Matthew 14:31* – "You of little faith, why did you doubt?"

2. **Waiting for Evidence Before Believing**

o Faith moves **before** results appear.

o If you wait to see, it's **not faith—it's sight**.

📖 Biblical Example: Thomas the Doubter (*John 20:24-29*) ✅ Thomas believed only after he saw Jesus' wounds. Jesus said, *"Blessed are those who have not seen and yet have believed."*

Practical Ways to Grow Mustard Seed Faith

1. **Read and Meditate on God's Word**

o Faith grows by **hearing the Word** (*Romans 10:17*).

2. **Surround Yourself With Faith Builders**

o Stay connected to believers **who encourage your faith**.

3. **Take Small Steps of Faith Daily**

o Faith is like a muscle—it grows **when exercised**.

4. **Speak God's Promises Over Your Life**

o Replace fear-filled thoughts with **faith-filled declarations**.

Faith in Action: Testimonies of Small Faith Producing Big Miracles

📖 Real-Life Testimony: A man with little money tithed in faith, believing God would provide. Within weeks, he received an unexpected financial blessing that changed his life.

📖 Historical Testimony: Smith Wigglesworth, a great man of faith, started with little knowledge of the Bible. But by taking small faith steps, he eventually prayed for the sick and saw miracles.

📖 Conclusion: Mustard Seed Faith Brings Great Results

📖 *Hebrews 11:6* – "Without faith, it is impossible to please God."

Faith doesn't need to be big—it just needs to be real. The mustard seed teaches us that even small faith moves mountains.

📖 Matthew 21:22 – "If you believe, you will receive whatever you ask for in prayer."

A small step of faith today can lead to a great breakthrough tomorrow. Are you willing to use the faith you have?

Faith is not about quantity but authenticity—and God can do the impossible with even the smallest seed of faith.

Chapter 8:
Faith in God's Promises

📖 *Hebrews 10:23* – "Let us hold unswervingly to the hope we profess, for He who promised is faithful."

Faith is **anchored in God's faithfulness**. Throughout Scripture, we see that God's promises never fail. Faith in His promises means trusting in His **timing, wisdom, and divine plan**, even when circumstances seem contrary.

Faith Anchored in God's Faithfulness

Believers often struggle with waiting on God's promises because they expect instant results. However, faith is about standing firm on God's Word before the fulfillment is visible.

📖 Biblical Example: Abraham and Sarah's Faith for a Child (Genesis 21:1-7) ✅ God promised Abraham that he would have descendants as numerous as the stars. Despite their old age, Abraham and Sarah held on to God's word, and Isaac was born in fulfillment of the promise.

📖 Romans 4:20-21 – "He did not waver through unbelief regarding the promise of God, but was strengthened in his faith and gave glory to God, being fully persuaded that God had power to do what He had promised."

Understanding God's Promises

1. **God's Promises Are Yes and Amen**

o   Every promise God makes is **certain** and **unchanging**.

o   His Word is the foundation of our **faith**.

📖 *2 Corinthians 1:20* – "For no matter how many promises God has made, they are 'Yes' in Christ."

2. **God's Promises Require Faith and Patience**

o   Faith means **trusting** God even when the promise **takes time**.

o   Many of God's greatest promises require **waiting and preparation**.

📖 Biblical Example: Joseph's Dreams (Genesis 37-50) ✅ Joseph had dreams of greatness, but he endured years of trials before God's promise was fulfilled.

Declaring Faith-Based Affirmations Aligns Believers with God's Word

📖 *Job 22:28* – "You will also decree a thing, and it will be established for you."

1. **Speak What God Has Spoken**

o   Declaring God's promises **reinforces faith**.

o   Faith-filled words align our thoughts with His will.

📖 Biblical Example: The Woman with the Issue of Blood (Mark 5:25-34) ✅ She declared in faith that if she touched Jesus' garment, she would be healed—and she was.

41

2. **Stand Firm Despite Delays**

o   God's promises often involve a **process**.

o   Faith trusts that **God is working** even when the answer isn't immediate.

📖 Biblical Example: The Israelites Entering the Promised Land (*Joshua 6:1-20*) ✅ They marched for seven days around Jericho before the walls fell. Faith persisted until the breakthrough came.

How to Strengthen Faith in God's Promises

1. Study and Meditate on His Promises

📖 *Romans 10:17* – "Faith comes by hearing, and hearing by the word of God."

• Knowing God's Word **increases faith**.
• His promises become **real** as we meditate on them.

2. Reject Fear and Doubt

📖 *Isaiah 41:10* – "Do not fear, for I am with you."

• Fear weakens faith.
• Doubt can prevent believers from receiving the promise.

📖 Biblical Example: Peter Walking on Water (*Matthew 14:28-31*) ✅ Peter stepped out in faith, but when he let doubt enter, he began to sink. Faith must remain focused on God.

3. Keep Praying and Expecting

📖 *Mark 11:24* – "Whatever you ask for in prayer, believe that you have received it, and it will be yours."

- Faith means praying and expecting without giving up.
- God's promises are received through persistent faith.

📖 Biblical Example: Hannah's Prayer for a Child (*1 Samuel 1:9-20*) ✅ Hannah prayed with unwavering faith, and God gave her Samuel, who became a great prophet.

Obstacles to Receiving God's Promises

1. **Impatience and Doubt**

o Many people **miss their promises** because they give up **too soon**.

📖 *Hebrews 6:12* – "Through faith and patience, we inherit the promises."

2. **Negative Words and Confession**

o Speaking **doubt and negativity** cancels faith.

o Always speak **God's truth**, even when circumstances seem opposite.

📖 Biblical Example: The Ten Spies and Their Bad Report (*Numbers 13:31-33*) ✅ Ten spies doubted and spoke fear, and they never entered the promised land. Faith must declare victory.

Faith in Action: Real-Life Testimonies

📖 Modern Testimony: A couple struggling with infertility declared God's promise of children over their lives. Despite medical reports, they stood in faith and conceived against the odds.

📖 Historical Testimony: George Müller ran orphanages by faith alone, never asking for money but always trusting God's provision. Every need was miraculously met.

📖 Conclusion: Faith in God's Promises Never Fails

📖 *Psalm 145:13* – "The Lord is trustworthy in all He promises and faithful in all He does."

Faith holds onto what God has spoken. His promises never fail—but they require faith, patience, and bold declaration.

📖 *Isaiah 55:11* – "So is my word that goes out from my mouth: It will not return to me empty but will accomplish what I desire."

Are you holding onto God's promises today?

The fulfillment of God's Word depends not on our strength, but on His faithfulness. Stand firm, speak life, and watch His promises come to pass.

Chapter 9:
Faith and Fear Cannot Coexist

📖 *Isaiah 41:10* – "Do not fear, for I am with you; do not be dismayed, for I am your God."

Faith and fear are opposites. Where faith grows, fear diminishes. Fear is the enemy of faith, causing hesitation, doubt, and spiritual paralysis. But the Bible repeatedly commands believers to "fear not" and to trust in God's power over circumstances.

Faith and Fear Cannot Rule the Same Heart

Faith is confidence in God's promises, while fear is confidence in the enemy's threats. When fear takes hold, it weakens our ability to walk in faith.

📖 Biblical Example: David Facing Goliath (1 Samuel 17) ✅ The Israelite army feared Goliath's size and threats, but David, full of faith in God, saw victory instead of defeat. Because he believed God's power was greater, fear did not control him.

📖 2 Timothy 1:7 – "For God has not given us a spirit of fear, but of power and of love and of a sound mind."

Fear Undermines Faith

1. Fear Focuses on the Problem, Faith Focuses on God

o Fear magnifies the obstacle. Faith magnifies God's ability to overcome it.

📖 Biblical Example: The Israelites at the Promised Land (Numbers 13:31-33) ✅ The ten spies focused on giants rather than God's promise, and fear robbed them of their inheritance.

📖 Psalm 56:3 – "When I am afraid, I put my trust in You."

2. Fear Paralyzes, Faith Moves Forward

o Fear causes hesitation, but faith acts on God's Word despite uncertainty.

📖 Biblical Example: Peter Walking on Water (Matthew 14:28-31) ✅ Peter walked by faith, but fear caused him to sink. Faith keeps the focus on Jesus, not the storm.

How to Eliminate Fear and Strengthen Faith

1. Trust God's Word Over Feelings

📖 *Isaiah 41:13* – "For I am the Lord your God who takes hold of your right hand and says to you, 'Do not fear; I will help you.'"

- Fear often comes from looking at circumstances.
- Faith declares God's truth despite emotions.

2. Speak Life, Not Fear

📖 *Proverbs 18:21* – "The tongue has the power of life and death."

- Speak faith-filled words, not words of fear and doubt.

📖 Biblical Example: Ezekiel Prophesying to Dry Bones (*Ezekiel 37:1-10*) ✅ Ezekiel spoke life, and dead bones came alive—our words impact reality.

3. Focus on God's Power, Not the Problem

📖 *Philippians 4:6-7* – "Do not be anxious about anything, but in every situation, by prayer and petition, with thanksgiving, present your requests to God."

- Replace worry with prayer.
- Faith flourishes in a heart that is fixed on God.

📖 Biblical Example: King Jehoshaphat's Battle (2 Chronicles 20:1-30) ✅ When Judah was surrounded, Jehoshaphat prayed and praised God in faith, and God fought the battle for them.

Fear Must Be Replaced With Faith

📖 *Joshua 1:9* – "Be strong and courageous. Do not be afraid; do not be discouraged, for the Lord your God will be with you wherever you go."

1. **Faith Requires Courage**

o Courage is not the absence of fear but choosing faith despite fear.

📖 Biblical Example: Esther's Bold Faith (*Esther 4:16*) ✅ Esther risked her life to save her people, declaring, *"If I perish, I perish."*

2. **Faith Brings Peace in Uncertainty**

o Fear creates turmoil. Faith rests in God's control.

📖 Biblical Example: Jesus Sleeping in the Storm (*Mark 4:35-41*) ✅ The disciples panicked, but Jesus rested in faith—He knew God was in control.

Practical Steps to Overcome Fear

1. **Meditate on God's Word**

o   Fill your mind with faith, not fear.

2. **Surround Yourself With Faith-Filled People**

o   Fear spreads. Stay with those who encourage faith.

3. **Take Steps of Faith Daily**

o   Faith is a **muscle**—it grows when used.

4. **Pray and Declare God's Promises Daily**

o   Fear shrinks when we speak faith into our situations.

📖 Biblical Example: Daniel in the Lion's Den (*Daniel 6:16-23*) ✅ Daniel trusted God, and his faith shut the mouths of lions.

Faith in Action: Real-Life Testimonies

📖 Modern Testimony: A man diagnosed with cancer refused to accept fear. He stood in faith, declared healing scriptures, and was miraculously healed.

📖 Historical Testimony: Corrie ten Boom, imprisoned during WWII, remained fearless in faith. Her trust in God impacted thousands.

📖 Conclusion: Faith and Fear Cannot Coexist

📖 Hebrews 11:6 – "Without faith, it is impossible to please God."

Fear and faith cannot live together. The more we trust in God, the less fear controls us.

📖 Psalm 23:4 – "Even though I walk through the valley of the shadow of death, I will fear no evil, for You are with me."

Faith chooses to trust God's promises even in the darkest moments. Are you choosing faith over fear today?

Chapter 10:
Faith in the Power of Prayer

📖 Mark 11:24 – "Whatever you ask for in prayer, believe that you have received it, and it will be yours."

Faith is essential for effective prayer. Many people pray, but not all believe they will receive what they ask for. Jesus teaches that prayer is not just about words—it must be rooted in faith. When we pray with unwavering belief, we align ourselves with God's power and promises.

The Connection Between Faith and Prayer

📖 Biblical Example: Elijah Praying for Rain (1 Kings 18:41-45)
✓ Elijah prayed persistently even when the sky was clear. He sent his servant seven times to check for rain before finally seeing a small cloud. His faith refused to give up.

📖 Hebrews 11:6 – "Without faith, it is impossible to please God."

1. **Prayer Without Faith is Empty Words**

o   Many people pray but doubt in their hearts.

o   Faith-filled prayer **expects results**.

📖 Biblical Example: The Prayer of Jabez (1 Chronicles 4:10) ✅ Jabez asked for blessing with bold faith, and God granted his request.

2. Faith-Filled Prayer Moves Mountains

o   Prayer is not begging God—it is aligning with His promises.

📖 Biblical Example: Joshua Commands the Sun to Stand Still (Joshua 10:12-14) ✅ Joshua prayed with faith, and God stopped the sun to give Israel victory.

Speaking Faith-Filled Prayers Aligns Us with God's Power

📖 *Job 22:28* – "You will also decree a thing, and it will be established for you."

1. Declare, Don't Just Request

o   Faith-filled prayer is speaking life into situations.

o   Jesus taught believers to speak to the mountain (*Mark 11:23*).

📖 Biblical Example: The Centurion's Faith (Matthew 8:5-13) ✅ The centurion said, "Just say the word, and my servant will be healed." His faith spoke the miracle into being.

2. Persistent Prayer Brings Breakthrough

o   Many give up when they don't see immediate results.

o   Faith persists until the promise is fulfilled.

📖 Biblical Example: The Persistent Widow (*Luke 18:1-8*) ✅ She refused to stop asking, and her persistence was rewarded.

How to Strengthen Faith in Prayer

1. Pray According to God's Will

📖 *1 John 5:14-15* – "If we ask anything according to His will, He hears us."

- Faith is strongest when our prayers align with God's Word.
- Study the Bible to pray God's promises, not just personal desires.

2. Reject Doubt and Fear

📖 *James 1:6* – "But when you ask, you must believe and not doubt."

- Doubt cancels faith.
- Expectation is key to answered prayer.

📖 Biblical Example: Bartimaeus' Bold Faith (Mark 10:46-52) ✔ He cried out for Jesus and refused to be silenced. His faith made him whole.

3. Speak Words of Faith Daily

📖 *Proverbs 18:21* – "The tongue has the power of life and death."

- Speak victory, healing, and provision.
- Negative words weaken faith.

📖 Biblical Example: Jesus Cursing the Fig Tree (Mark 11:12-14, 20-24) ✔ Jesus spoke, and the tree withered—demonstrating the power of spoken faith.

Overcoming Obstacles to Faith in Prayer

1. Praying Without Expectation

o   Many people hope but don't believe.

o   Faith-filled prayer expects a result.

📖 *Matthew 21:22* – "If you believe, you will receive whatever you ask for in prayer."

2. Giving Up Too Soon

o   Some prayers require persistence.

o   Delay does not mean denial.

📖 **Biblical Example:** Daniel's 21-Day Prayer (*Daniel 10:12-14*)
✓ The answer was **sent immediately**, but resistance in the spiritual realm delayed it.

Faith in Prayer Produces Miracles

📖 Modern Testimony: A woman prayed for her prodigal son for years. She never stopped believing, and one day, he gave his life to Christ.

📖 Historical Testimony: Smith Wigglesworth prayed bold prayers, and thousands were healed by faith.

📖 Conclusion: Faith and Prayer Cannot Be Separated

📖 *Luke 11:9* – "Ask, and it will be given to you; seek, and you will find; knock, and the door will be opened to you."

Faith-filled prayer produces supernatural results. When believers pray with faith, mountains move, lives change, and miracles happen.

📖 *Ephesians 3:20* – "Now to Him who is able to do immeasurably more than all we ask or imagine."

Are you praying with faith or just saying words? It's time to believe, declare, and expect God to move!

Chapter 11:
Faith from God's Perspective

📖 *Hebrews 11:6* – "Without faith, it is impossible to please God."

From My eternal throne, I have ordained faith as the foundation of My relationship with humanity. Faith is not simply a concept; it is the **spiritual force** that activates My will in the earth. Without faith, My promises remain unfulfilled in a believer's life, not because I withhold, but because faith is the key that unlocks divine realities. Faith is the currency of heaven—without it, you cannot transact in the supernatural.

Faith Activates Divine Realities

Faith is the bridge between the unseen and the seen, between what I have declared and what you experience. My Word is eternal, but without faith, it does not manifest in your life.

📖 Biblical Example: Abraham's Faith (Genesis 15:6) ✓ Abraham believed My promise of descendants, and his faith was counted as righteousness. His faith activated My covenant.

📖 Romans 4:17 – "I have made you a father of many nations. He is our father in the sight of God, in whom he believed—the God who gives life to the dead and calls into being things that were not."

1. **Faith Calls Things That Are Not Into Existence**

o   I created the world through faith—by speaking what was not yet seen (*Hebrews 11:3*).

o   When you speak My promises in faith, you align with My creative power.

📖 Biblical Example: Ezekiel's Prophecy Over Dry Bones (Ezekiel 37:1-10) ✅ Ezekiel spoke life over dry bones, and My Spirit breathed life into them. Faith speaks into the void and creates.

2. **Faith is Beyond Human Understanding**

• My ways are higher than yours (*Isaiah 55:8-9*).
• Faith is not based on sight but on trust in My Word.

📖 Biblical Example: The Walls of Jericho (Joshua 6:1-20) ✅ Marching in silence made no sense, but faith produced the miracle.

Why Faith Pleases Me

📖 *Hebrews 11:1* – "Now faith is the substance of things hoped for, the evidence of things not seen."

Faith pleases Me because it proves that you trust **who I AM** more than what you see. It is the highest form of worship because it acknowledges My sovereignty, My power, and My absolute faithfulness.

1. **Faith Demonstrates Total Dependence on Me**

o   You cannot please Me without faith because faith means you trust in My love and My ability to sustain you.

📖 Biblical Example: Daniel in the Lions' Den (*Daniel 6:22*) ✅ He did not fear the lions because his faith was in My deliverance.

2. **Faith is the Foundation of My Kingdom**

o My kingdom operates on faith—every miracle in Scripture happened through faith.

📖 Biblical Example: The Woman with the Issue of Blood (*Mark 5:25-34*) ✅ She received healing because her faith pulled virtue from My Son.

What Hinders Faith?

Faith is often hindered by doubt, fear, and reliance on human reasoning. When you struggle with faith, it is because you are **looking at the natural** instead of **trusting in My eternal Word**.

1.Doubt Cancels Faith

📖 *James 1:6-7* – "The one who doubts is like a wave of the sea, blown and tossed by the wind. That person should not expect to receive anything from the Lord."

📖 Biblical Example: Peter Walking on Water (Matthew 14:28-31) ✅ He walked by faith, but when he doubted, he began to sink. Doubt weakens faith.

2.Fear Replaces Faith

📖 *2 Timothy 1:7* – "For God has not given us a spirit of fear, but of power, love, and a sound mind."

📖 Biblical Example: The Israelites at the Promised Land (*Numbers 13:31-33*) ✅ Fear kept them from My promise. Faith sees victory; fear sees obstacles.

How to See from My Perspective

1. Fix Your Eyes on the Unseen

📖 *2 Corinthians 4:18* – "We fix our eyes not on what is seen, but on what is unseen."

- Faith requires focusing on My promises **over circumstances**.
- When you see with **spiritual eyes**, you recognize that My reality is greater than what you experience in the natural.

📖 Biblical Example: Elisha's Servant (2 Kings 6:15-17) ✅ Elisha prayed for his servant's eyes to be opened, and he saw My angel armies surrounding them. Faith sees beyond the visible.

2. Speak My Word with Authority

📖 *Isaiah 55:11* – "My word… will not return to Me empty, but will accomplish what I desire."

- Faith grows as you declare My Word.
- Every time you speak My promises, you release My power into your situation.

📖 Biblical Example: Jesus Speaking to the Fig Tree (Mark 11:12-14, 20-24) ✅ Jesus cursed the tree, and it withered—faith speaks and expects results.

Faith Prepares You for Greater Glory

📖 Romans 1:17 – "The righteous shall live by faith."

Faith is not just for momentary breakthroughs—it is a lifestyle. I call you to live every day by faith, trusting Me completely.

📖 Biblical Example: Noah's Faith (Hebrews 11:7) ✅ Noah built the ark before rain had ever existed. His faith prepared him for a future only I could see.

1. Faith Brings You into Supernatural Realities

o When you operate in faith, you experience My supernatural provision and power.

📖 Biblical Example: Manna in the Wilderness (Exodus 16:4-36) ✅ The Israelites had to trust Me daily for provision.

2. Faith Leads to Eternal Reward

o Faith is not just about what you see now—it is about your eternal inheritance.

📖 John 14:1-2 – "Do not let your hearts be troubled. You believe in God; believe also in Me. My Father's house has many rooms."

📖 Biblical Example: The Faith of the Martyrs (Hebrews 11:35-40) ✅ Many were persecuted, yet they held onto faith because they saw My eternal reward.

Conclusion: Faith is the Key to My Kingdom

📖 Luke 18:8 – "When the Son of Man comes, will He find faith on the earth?"

Faith is the key to everything I have for you. Without it, you cannot please Me. But with faith, you can move mountains, receive promises, and walk in My divine will.

📖 *Habakkuk 2:4* – "The just shall live by faith."

Will you trust Me completely? Will you walk by faith and not by sight? Faith is more than belief—it is the living connection between you and My divine plan. Step into faith, and you will see My glory revealed.

Chapter 12:
Faith and Salvation—The Role of Jesus and the Holy Spirit

📖 Ephesians 2:8-9 – "For it is by grace you have been saved, through faith—and this is not from yourselves, it is the gift of God—not by works, so that no one can boast."

Faith is the foundation of salvation. Without faith in Jesus Christ, no one can receive eternal life. Faith is the bridge between God's gift of grace and human redemption. It is not merely believing that God exists, but trusting in the finished work of Jesus Christ and allowing the Holy Spirit to transform the heart.

Faith in Christ is Essential for Salvation

📖 Biblical Example: The Thief on the Cross (Luke 23:39-43) ✅ One thief mocked Jesus, while the other expressed faith, saying, "Remember me when You come into Your kingdom." Jesus responded, "Truly I tell you, today you will be with Me in paradise."

This thief had no chance for works, but his faith alone granted him eternal life. Faith is not about what we do—it is about trusting in what Christ has already done.

📖 Romans 10:9 – "If you declare with your mouth, 'Jesus is Lord,' and believe in your heart that God raised Him from the dead, you will be saved."

1. **Salvation Comes Only Through Faith in Jesus**

o   Good deeds cannot **earn salvation**.

o   Only faith in Jesus' death and resurrection brings **forgiveness of sins**.

📖 Biblical Example: The Philippian Jailer (Acts 16:30-31) ✅ He asked, "What must I do to be saved?" Paul replied, "Believe in the Lord Jesus, and you will be saved."

2. **Faith Leads to Transformation**

o   True faith changes lives—it is not passive.

o   Salvation by faith produces spiritual fruit (*Galatians 5:22-23*).

📖 Biblical Example: Zacchaeus' Faith (Luke 19:1-10) ✅ Zacchaeus' faith in Jesus led him to repent and restore what he had stolen. Faith produces action.

The Role of the Holy Spirit in Strengthening Faith

📖 *John 16:13* – "When the Spirit of truth comes, He will guide you into all truth."

The Holy Spirit does more than seal believers for salvation—He strengthens faith, teaches truth, and empowers believers to walk by faith.

1. **The Holy Spirit Convicts and Draws People to Faith**

📖 *John 16:8* – "When He comes, He will convict the world concerning sin and righteousness and judgment."

•   No one can come to **faith in Jesus** without the work of the Holy Spirit.

📖 Biblical Example: Saul's Conversion to Paul (Acts 9:1-19) ✅ Saul persecuted Christians until Jesus appeared to him and the Holy Spirit transformed his heart.

2. The Holy Spirit Strengthens Faith in Trials

📖 *2 Corinthians 12:9* – "My grace is sufficient for you, for My power is made perfect in weakness."

• When faith is **tested**, the Holy Spirit gives **strength** to endure.

📖 **Biblical Example:** Stephen's Faith Under Persecution (*Acts 7:54-60*) ✅ As he was stoned, **Stephen saw Jesus in heaven** and remained faithful until death.

Faith is Not Just for Salvation—It is a Daily Walk

📖 Galatians 2:20 – "I have been crucified with Christ and I no longer live, but Christ lives in me. The life I now live in the body, I live by faith in the Son of God."

Faith does not end at salvation—it is the foundation of daily Christian life. Faith must be lived out.

📖 Biblical Example: Peter Walking in Daily Faith (Matthew 16:15-18) ✅ Peter confessed that Jesus was the Christ, and his faith became the foundation of the Church.

1.Faith Requires Daily Trust in God

📖 *Matthew 6:33* – "Seek first the kingdom of God and His righteousness, and all these things will be added to you."

• Faith is about trusting God's provision and guidance.
• Daily faith means relying on God instead of worry and fear.

📖 Biblical Example: Manna in the Wilderness (Exodus 16:4) ✅ The Israelites had to trust God daily for their food.

2. **Faith Empowers Prayer and Miracles**

📖 *James 5:15* – "The prayer of faith will save the sick, and the Lord will raise them up."

- Faith allows believers to pray boldly and expect results.

📖 Biblical Example: The Persistent Widow (Luke 18:1-8) ✅ She kept praying, and her faith led to breakthrough.

Overcoming Doubt and Strengthening Faith

Faith is often challenged, but doubt can be overcome.

1. **Feed Faith with the Word of God**

📖 *Romans 10:17* – "Faith comes by hearing, and hearing by the word of God."

📖 Biblical Example: The Bereans (Acts 17:11) ✅ They searched the Scriptures to strengthen their faith.

2. **Walk in Obedience, Even When It's Hard**

📖 *Hebrews 10:38* – "The righteous shall live by faith."

- Faith grows when it is put into action.
- Obedience builds trust in God's faithfulness.

📖 Biblical Example: Abraham Offering Isaac (Genesis 22:1-18) ✅ Abraham obeyed, and his faith brought blessing.

Faith Leads to Eternal Life

📖 *John 3:16* – "For God so loved the world that He gave His one and only Son, that whoever believes in Him shall not perish but have eternal life."

1. Faith is the Key to Heaven

o   Without faith in Jesus, **eternal life is impossible**.

o   Faith in Christ secures **our eternal home**.

📖 Biblical Example: The Rich Young Ruler (Matthew 19:16-22)
✓ He believed in God, but lacked faith to surrender fully.

2. Faith Keeps Us Focused on the Eternal

📖 *Colossians 3:2* – "Set your minds on things above, not on earthly things."

•   Faith is not just about this life—it prepares us for eternity.

📖 Biblical Example: The Martyrs in Revelation (Revelation 12:11) ✓ They overcame by the blood of the Lamb and the word of their testimony.

Conclusion: Faith is the Lifeline of Salvation

📖 2 Timothy 4:7 – "I have fought the good fight, I have finished the race, I have kept the faith."

Faith begins at salvation, continues in our daily walk, and is perfected in eternity. Without faith, no one can please God, receive His grace, or enter into eternal life.

📖 Hebrews 12:2 – "Fixing our eyes on Jesus, the pioneer and perfecter of faith."

Are you walking by faith daily? Are you trusting in Jesus not just for salvation but for every aspect of life?

Faith in Christ is the foundation of everything. Live by faith, and you will see God's glory revealed.

www.ingramcontent.com/pod-product-compliance
Lightning Source LLC
LaVergne TN
LVHW052037080426
835513LV00018B/2367